# You're Not Broken

What Jesus Really Said and Why it Matters

Stephen Fofanoff

ZAMIZ PRESS

Categories: RELIGION > INSPIRATIONAL
RELIGION > CHRISTIAN THEOLOGY > LIBERATION

Special discounts are available on quantity purchases by corporations, associations and others. For details, contact the author.

The information in this book is not intended to replace the advice of a physician. It is for informational purposes only and any supplement, diet, or exercise program should be started under the advisement of a physician.

Neither the author nor the publisher assumes any responsibility or liability whatsoever on behalf of the consumer or reader of this material. Any perceived slight of any individual or organization is purely unintentional.

DO YOU HAVE A MESSAGE TO SHARE WITH THE WORLD?
ARE YOU INTERESTED IN HAVING YOUR BOOK PUBLISHED?
VISIT ZAMIZPRESS.COM

All rights reserved. No part of this publication may be reproduced, distributed or transmitted in any form or by any means, including photocopying, recording, or other electronic or mechanical methods, without the prior written permission of the publisher, except in the case of brief quotations embodied in critical reviews and certain other noncommercial uses permitted by copyright law.

Quotes from *The Unvarnished New Testament: A New Translation From The Original Greek* by Andy Gaus, published in 1991 by Phanes Press.

Copyright © 2021 by Stephen Fofanoff

Cover Design by Alexander Von Ness

You're Not Broken: What Jesus Really Said and Why it Matters — 2$^{nd}$ Edition
ISBN: 978-1-949813-12-8

To the askers and the seekers.
This book is for everyone.
Hopefully, you can find something that uplifts you
and builds up your spirit within its pages.

Look in your heart, for there you will find glory.

# ACKNOWLEDGMENTS

This work wouldn't be possible without the love and support of my family and friends: Chris, you are my rock. Mom and Dad, you are my safety net. Audrey and Stephanie, a lifetime of friendship is not enough. Carlos, your personal success is an inspiration. To the many clients I've helped through the years, thank you for teaching me more than I have given you. Finally, to Andy Gaus, we've never met, but your translation of the Gospels broke open the message of Jesus in ways no other could. Thank you.

*"Ask and you will receive,
look and you will find,
knock and you will be admitted.
For the asker always gets,
the seeker finds,
and whoever knocks is admitted."*

*- The Good Word According to Matthew,
Chapter Seven*

# Contents

Chapter 1: Guilt Surrounds Us ........................................................ 1
Chapter 2: We've Been Down This Road Before ...................... 11
Chapter 3: Where's Christ in Today's Christianity? ................. 17
Chapter 4: What Jesus Really Said About God ....................... 27
Chapter 5: What Jesus Really Said About People .................... 31
Chapter 6: What Jesus Really Said About Salvation ................ 35
Chapter 7: What Jesus Really Said About Religion .................. 39
Chapter 8: How To Live An Un-Broken Life With Yourself .... 45
Chapter 9: How To Live An Un-Broken Life With Others ....... 53
Chapter 10: Why It Still Matters ................................................. 59
Chapter 11: Applying the Word to Today ................................. 65
FOCUS: Politics ........................................................................... 65
FOCUS: Value Of Life ................................................................. 69
FOCUS: Sexuality ........................................................................ 73
FOCUS: Environment ................................................................. 77

FOCUS: Science ................................................................. 79

FOCUS: Salvation ............................................................. 81

FOCUS: Evangelism ......................................................... 83

About the Author ............................................................. 85

# INTRODUCTION

What if Christianity only had the four gospels? What if Christians used the actual words and actions of Jesus as their only means of understanding their relationship with God and other people? This book examines what Christianity means when Jesus is the only lens, and then what it means when that lens is placed within the context of our contemporary world. No old Law. No new Law. No attempting to "balance" conflicts between the Old and New Testaments, no Paul, no epistles, no Book of Revelation. Just Jesus, His life, His teachings, His words and actions. By asking the question of what Christianity looks like when the layers are removed, the filters are eliminated, and Jesus is viewed as not only the beginning and the end (the Alpha and Omega), but as the Only, we get to see what pure Christianity looks like. And it looks very different from the Christianity we've come to accept in our country, our churches, and our lives.

This book is about our relationship with the divine and with ourselves I want to make a few notes here at the beginning to be sure we're all on the same page and have a common understanding of what this book is, why it's written, and what the intentions are.

This book isn't here to convince or convert anyone to my way of thinking. If you happen to read this and feel enlightened, that's great. If reading this and you feel enraged, I don't expect everyone will agree with everything I've written. I hope you are able to take these things that seem to fit in your life and leave behind whatever doesn't. I'll have no hard feelings either way.

More and more people are misunderstanding the fundamental message of Jesus. This isn't anything new, but it has become strikingly apparent to me over the past couple of decades in America. After years of searching for someone else who was saying what I believe to be true, I tired of searching and decided to say it myself.

A friend of mine said that she believes some people don't have a choice in their lives because they are broken. Through depression, chemical imbalance or other illness, they are in a particular situation where they do not have the free will to choose something other than what they are currently experiencing in their lives.

I agree with her in that there are some people who choose not to have a choice. They choose to embrace whatever situation they find themselves in. They choose not to seek medical attention or assistance from others. They choose to remain in their state of depression or illness and believe they are a victim of whatever circumstances they find themselves in.

We all have a choice. The choices I talk about are not ones that I can, will or should make for you. Those choices are up to you, through careful counsel, consideration and perhaps even prayer to do what is right for you. The first step to that will be accepting personal responsibility for yourself, your life, and your future. The past is already written, and there is nothing you can do about it except to move on. The future is not yet written and cannot be determined. But you do own the present moment, completely and fully. In this present moment, every choice you make will determine what happens next.

I have extensively studied scripture and the life of Jesus. I may reference scripture or Jesus, but I will do so generally, to showcase the spirit of the message. There are many books that provide specific quotes and academic accolades to justify their work. I will not be citing chapter and verse nor will I be seeking academic validation. Instead, I hope to bring the message of Jesus to life for today's times. I intentionally forgo all of those trappings, footnotes and bibliographies to engage in a conversation with you. This is about creating a living relationship with Jesus starting now.

I have chosen to use the text from "The Unvarnished Gospels," as translated by Andy Gaus. George Witterschein makes this statement about Andy Gaus's translation: "As is so often the case, defensiveness leads to impoverishment. It is Andy Gaus's good fortune—and the reader's—that he is not defending a body of [Church] doctrine. He is just translating as faithfully as he can, like the good German-American Midwesterner he was raised to be." I encourage you to pick up a copy of "The Unvarnished Gospels" yourself to read the English translations of the Greek texts in as close to their original, as you can. With no regard for church doctrine, just a loving regard for the original words and their deepest meanings, the text should guide our beliefs, not the other way around.

My hope, though, is that through this book, you discover the true message of Jesus for yourself without all of the politics and religion that seems to get in the way of it. It is truly a message that can transform your life in powerful ways, if you open your mind and heart.

Every blessing,
Stephen

# 1

# GUILT SURROUNDS US

*"Woe to you...*
*for being like dusty monuments*
*that look pretty on the outside*
*but on the inside are full of the*
*bones of corpses and all kinds of rot.*
*You likewise from the outside*
*appear to the world to be decent,*
*but inside you're full of hypocrisy*
*and ways around the law."*

The Good Word According to Matthew,
Chapter Twenty-Three

As young children, many of us learned to embrace guilt, to own it fully as the foundation of our lives. At the dinner table, we learn that—even though we are full—people are starving everywhere and we should feel bad because we have food and they don't. And so, we should overfill ourselves and learn unhealthy eating habits because others haven't enough. We learn that we should feel guilt when we are experiencing the joys of life, because after all we have to learn to grow up sometime.

Being an adult we're taught means that we do not have child-like joy – no more wonder and amazement at the magnificence of our existence. Instead, we are told to feel guilty whenever we feel good, especially because we know that someone else in the world does not feel good. We're told that we should never feel better than anyone else. We also learn that we should not receive more than anyone else; or if we do at least that we should feel guilty about it. We learn to speak of "guilty pleasures" as though anything that is pleasurable in life should be experienced with guilt. And our daily language has adapted to reflect this unspoken view of the world.

Life, it seems, is supposed to be a struggle. We're meant to "overcome and triumph" over the many challenges, problems, and troubles we'll face every day. We forget one of the foundations of Jesus' message.

*"Come here to me, all you drudges and overburdened ones, and I will give you rest. Put my yoke on and learn from me: I am gentle and humble of heart, and you will find rest for your souls, because my yoke is kindly and my load is light."*

The Good Word According to Matthew,
Chapter Eleven

The trouble is that God never intended for us to live a challenging life. Jesus tells us that God wants us to live lives filled with joy, love, peace and abundance. And, in fact, has already provided us with everything we need to have that life. The universe is literally built around this concept – to actively say "yes" to everything we need and desire. And we report to God in every moment exactly what we desire, which is to receive more and more of whatever we focus on. And we focus on a lot of things. Unfortunately, we've learned to focus on fear and scarcity. And so the universe brings more and more of that into our lives. When we feel guilty, we are brought ever more into a world where we should feel guilty. In other words, the more we focus on these feelings, the more our reality will shift to match it.

Do you feel guilty about overeating? Do you have too much food? Do you have wonderful desserts? With such a focus, you're sure to be given a reality that matches. You are sure to gain weight, and to feel more guilt and shame as a result. And when you feel more guilt and shame, you'll eat more, and you'll make poorer eating choices, you'll find yourself at your favorite fast food restaurant more often, which results in gaining more weight and feeling more guilt. And the cycle will continue.

Imagine, instead, that you feel no guilt; secure in the knowledge that you treat your body well. With such a focus, you're sure to be given a reality that matches. You might skip dessert or listen to your body and stop eating a few bites sooner. That might lead to eating a healthier choice at your next meal, or skipping a sugary drink. These healthier choices will result in losing weight or improving your health in other ways. And this new cycle will continue with improved health and vitality.

You can always make a shift back to your desired reality. And the first step on that road is to eliminate the guilt and shame you've learned to live with (or for). You have to reclaim God's love and happiness in your life. You have to live with feelings associated with a lighter being. And your reality will shift to match those feelings. It is not magic. It is the way that God built the world. Just as there are physical laws, there are also spiritual laws that work in conjunction with those physical laws. You don't have to understand the law of gravity to be affected by it, and you don't have to understand any of the spiritual laws to know that they are working every day in your life.

## Turn the Other Cheek

How often do you get angry? I'm talking about real self-righteous anger. The kind where you know you are absolutely right.

You have every right to be angry. You were "wronged." You were cut off in traffic. Someone cut in front of you in line. The "automated voice response system" at the bank/company/store keeps disconnecting you or transferring you to the wrong department. Your time is being wasted. Your heart is broken. In short, your anger is a righteous anger. And you have every right to it.

You are correct. You have every right to be angry. But, should you? Should you drain all of your energy into your anger? Should you push all of your consciousness into anger? Should you drive your intuitive mind into anger? Should you consume your soul with anger?

I'm not suggesting for a moment that anger is a bad thing. I'm just pointing out that we often have a choice to be angry or not. Sure, anger is a feeling that we seem to have little control over. It comes up when we don't expect it. And my point here is that we can choose whether or not to be consumed by anger, or we can choose to understand the anger, move through it, and heal what really caused it. No one else is the cause of our anger; we have to own it.

Anger is a response mechanism that we experience when our beliefs have been violated – "I should have been treated with more respect in this situation" or "I trusted this person and my trust has been violated." There are perhaps many other beliefs that can be violated to the point of anger.

Jesus got angry. He overturned the tables. He screamed. "Not in my Father's house!" We know anger is a part of the human condition. And it should not be ignored. We should never bottle up our anger. When Jesus got angry, he understood what belief had been violated, and he acted on his anger. Sometimes we have to act on our anger as well, but we know that there will be a cost for acting on anger—especially when we don't fully understand where it comes from and what belief has been violated in our life. Anger comes from fear, jealousy and shame.

Jesus was angry at the religious leaders who had led people away from God – religious leaders who believed that rules and regulations were more important than a relationship with God...religious leaders who thought it was ok to turn a sacred place where people were supposed to come to offer their own sacrifice and to be with God into a bank and marketplace. Yet today, how many church leaders spend their time asking for money? They seem to spend all their time writing books titled "How God Will Give You Lots of Money IF You Donate To My Church?"

Jesus was angry because these were people who knew better. They knew what God wanted, and they chose to do something else. They chose to put their own needs first. They thought the church—the institution—was more important than God. They thought they could put God in a box or a building or a law. But Jesus knew that God is bigger than the box, the building, and the law. Jesus was willing to die because God loves everyone and wants every human being to experience that love firsthand.

Outside of that, Jesus recognized that anger was something to let go of. Jesus wasn't consumed with anger even at the temple leaders. How often do we hold on to our anger? How many times do we retell the stories of how we are wronged? How many times do we relive each painful memory? We have a choice in each moment to embrace a thought or feeling or to let it go. The reality is that our minds cannot hold on to more than one thought in a specific instance. Our minds chaotically wander from one thought to the next, in a battle between consciousness and intuition. Yet when we embark on the path of wholeness, our conscious and intuitive minds become synchronized.

This synchronization allows us to let go of those negative thoughts and feelings while still acknowledging that they are present. We can experience the anger, move through it, and understand it. We know what the beliefs are that need to be changed versus the beliefs that are so sacred we are willing to die for them. We can put our anger into perspective and neither live within it nor be consumed by it. In other words, we can let it go because we know that we live in harmony with God.

God has structured the universe to work for us when we tune in our conscious and intuitive minds to the energy of God's love. When we believe that God loves us, cares for us, and provides for us, we act differently within the universe. And the universe responds by creating circumstances that reinforce those beliefs for us.

When we embrace anger and allow it to consume us, or when we embrace loneliness, despair, "brokenness," and sadness, we are asking the universe to create circumstances that will reinforce those feelings. Jesus said that whatever we believe about something, it will be true. If we choose to let something go, it is gone. If we choose to hold on to something, it will remain. The most amplified of these feelings are shame and guilt.

Guilt and shame seem to be the two main feelings that most religious leaders base their churches on. Shame and guilt are good, they say. These are the things that make us realize that we are hell-bound, evil, unworthy specks within a grand universe of God's judgment. We are outside of God's love, they tell us, and we must repent. We must embrace the guilt and shame and use them as tools to remind us of "who we really are."

Quite frankly, that's just crap. It's a question of which came first. God never intended for us to live lives filled with guilt and shame. The vast majority of guilt and shame come from our lack of experience outside of ourselves. We somehow believe that we are unique in our individual experience. We are the only ones who think these things, feel these things, act this way. We are the only ones who struggle with whatever we have labeled our "internal demons." The reality is, however, that we are not really that unique.

Religious leaders would have us think otherwise. They tell us that who we are is fundamentally wrong. We're broken. And we need to be fixed. What is the fix? "Deny yourself, and join my church." But that isn't quite what Jesus said. We are supposed to deny ourselves, take up our cross, and follow him. But what does that mean exactly? Let's look at it more closely.

To deny yourself in contemporary Christian terms today means to change who you are, to suffer and sacrifice for Christ. But is that really what Jesus meant? I don't think so. Instead, look at it this way. At the core of the human experience is the desire to be more than human, to never be satisfied with who we are or what we have. Our egos are larger than we are. But when we deny our egos, and instead we focus on who we are and what we have—when we live in reality—we get a different picture. We are able to realize that God has given us everything we need. Our egos can get in the way of our relationship with God.

To deny ourselves is to deny our egos, to allow ourselves to live in God's love. We are given the ability to recognize God's love more fully in our lives. We are not subject to our ego's demands that we should remain unsettled and in doubt. To deny ourselves is to let go of jealousy, envy, and possession. When we deny ourselves, we live in harmony with God. We live in God's grace.

To take up your cross in contemporary Christianity is to live with the shame and guilt that are associated with whatever "sin" we are facing. Generally, taking up your cross seems to be about trying to avoid your "sinful nature" however you can. "My cross is my quick temper." "My cross is my loneliness." "My cross is this horrible relationship I have with my parents." "My cross is having to stand in this long line."

How did Jesus take up his cross and what was it exactly?

Jesus' cross was his destiny. His cross was, literally, the means to salvation. His cross was his entire purpose for coming to the earth to live among us. He understood his cross as his mission in this life. Jesus did not walk away from his cross, nor did he view it as a bad thing, as a "necessary evil." Jesus embraced it fully. He understood that he was living within God's love, and that everyone has value and purpose. His value and purpose was to share the good news that God loves everyone—that no one is outside of God's love. And he did not try to hide that from anyone.

How often do we try to hide our cross today? Our cross—our mission and reason for being on this planet—is the thing we are supposed to take up for all to see. God has given each of us unique gifts, talents and abilities. God has given each of us tremendous value. And we are supposed to fulfill our destinies. Instead, we live in fear or who we are and what we are called to do. We allow religious leaders to drive us away from God's purpose for us to raise up human institutions and make them more important than God. They tell us that the way to serve God is to serve their church. Yet, Jesus tells us that no one can serve two masters. Think of "the cross" as a banner to waive high.

- Do you have the gift of singing?
- Do you have the gift of healing?
- Do you have the gift of true leadership?
- Do you have the gift of creativity?

- Do you have the gift of intuition?
- Do you have the gift of relating well to others?
- Do you have the gift of organization?

Carry those crosses! Don't hide your true purpose and gifts from others. Your cross, your life's purpose, is significant, and only you can carry it. Don't allow anyone else to tell you to hide it.

To follow Jesus in modern Christianity is generally to belong to the church of the person who is telling you to follow Jesus. It seems Christians can't agree on exactly which is the right way to follow Jesus and so they spend all of their time trying to determine why another church is wrong and theirs is right. I've never understood why church leaders have determined that their job—their main function—is to judge others as either "worthy" or "unworthy"—or put a different way, "saved" and "unsaved."

"For humans, nothing is possible, but for God, all things are possible."

God, you'll remember, is bigger than any church, any interpretation of the Bible, any dogmatic principle. God is, well, God. And we are not. No church leader is God. I am not God. You are not God. But, we are all within God's love. What would the world look like if all Christians followed Jesus instead of following a particular church? What would happen if all people realized they were loved fully and completely. What would the world look like if everyone trusted in God to provide?

Greed, envy, and jealousy are all by-products of a lack of belief in God's love and abundance. If I truly believe that God loves and cares for me, then why would I be jealous of what someone else has? I would have no need to judge myself as lacking anything. I would recognize that my life is an amazing gift and I would choose to embrace that every day. I would make every day the best it can be. I would recognize that God gives me everything I need for today. I have no need to live in the past or the future because there is so much to live for today.

## Take a Moment

⇒ Imagine yourself completely and totally loved. No conditions. No strings. Just bathed in love and acceptance. Like a Big Hug that never ends. Spend some time in that hug. Drink it in with all of your senses.

⇒ Did you experience resistance or a nagging voice that tried to convince you that you weren't worthy of love? That you should feel guilty if you accept the hug?

⇒ If so, where does that voice come from? Move through the resistance to understand why you reject parts of yourself. Ultimately, any resistance you experience has been "programmed" into your consciousness. The more you try to reason with the "Voice," the more power you give it. Embrace the Voice and allow it to experience love and acceptance without questioning it.

⇒ Try this exercise every day for as long as you are able. If you find yourself outside of the experience, simply shift your focus back to the Big Hug, even if for a few seconds at a time.

# 2

# WE'VE BEEN DOWN THIS ROAD BEFORE

*And he said to them,*
*"You're the kind who justifies yourselves*
*in the eyes of the world.*
*But God knows your hearts:*
*what is sublime to the world*
*is a horror in the eyes of God."*

The Good Word According to Luke,
Chapter Sixteen

Today, religious leaders spend an awful lot of time trying to determine who is welcome within a community and who is not. Roles, rules and codes seem to define religions today. Every church will tell you who's "in" and who's "out." And they can probably do that better than focusing on true spiritual truths that challenge the very foundations of most churches today. There is a spoken and pervasive obsession with

"The Law." In some churches, it almost overshadows everything else.

To understand the message of Jesus, we have to put it into the context of his life. Jesus lived in a specific time period and in a specific geography. His teachings were specific to the community of believers to whom he spoke and with whom He lived. To ignore that entirely is to ignore Jesus' own teaching that God is a dynamic being who adapts and changes according to the needs of the people who are alive today. Who was he and why did he say the things he said the way that he said them?

If you are unfamiliar with the life of Jesus, here's a brief overview. Sometime about the year 6 to 4 BCE (or B.C.), Jesus was born in what is now modern-day Israel, in a small town called Bethlehem. Sometime around the year 24 to 26 CE (or A.D.), Jesus engaged in what would become a three-year ministry among the Jewish people before being crucified by the Roman authorities with the assistance of some religious and political leaders of the local area. Crucifixion was a common way of enacting the death penalty for certain crimes in the Roman Empire.

The Jewish leadership of the day was divided into predominantly two groups: Sadducees and Pharisees. Jesus spoke about both during his brief period of ministry. He gathered about himself a small group of followers, everyday people who for the first time heard a message of hope and inspiration that would forever change their lives.

You see the religious leadership of the Jewish people believed a few things about God:

- God was a single God, apparently among many other gods of the time that were embraced by other people living among and around the Jews.

- This God specifically choose the Jewish people to have a

special relationship with.

- God gave the Jews a set of laws that would determine and define the relationship because the people asked for the law.

- To be among the "chosen people," you would have to follow the specific laws set out in this covenant.

- God would protect you and reciprocate the relationship if you followed the laws.

In other words, the laws defined who was "in" the community and who was "out." It determined social and religious ranking. It was a specific attempt to define the community. And it worked very well doing just that.

Every community, especially religious ones, has a code that defines the membership of the group, including what is expected of group members. Nations have laws that govern citizenship. Religions have laws that govern participation and inclusion within the group. The religious leaders of Jesus' time were no different in this regard. They enforced the law to the best of their ability.

Before Jesus, religious teachers within the Jewish community always supported the law and the religious leadership in their efforts to enforce it. Those leaders and prophets strengthened the special relationship between the Jewish people and God.

But Jesus offered a different message. Here is the short version of his teachings: God created, loves, and cares for everyone regardless of their strict adherence to the law (and so non-Jews were included in this group). But Jesus took this a step further, indicating that the religious leaders were so much more concerned about the law and defining who was "accepted" and who was "shunned" by the community that they neglected the people's relationship with God. Jesus indicated that individual people can and should have a direct relationship with God.

This is not to say that Jesus completely rejected religion and religious activities. Instead, he put them within the context of the individual's connection with God. No religion or religious leader could get in the way of that direct connection. But religious leaders could certainly help to cultivate it. But what's so special about that? People have been saying that for years, and they don't necessarily have major religions based on them or their teachings.

The key was understanding the fundamental meaning of Jesus' message. This simple, life-transforming message that, when applied today, can continue to transform lives, improve communities, and change the world. It can, literally, bring about world peace and transformation.

But what is this message and why is it so life-transforming? And why don't more people talk about it? Why aren't Christian leaders shouting this message from the mountaintops? Why isn't the message sweeping across the land?

Because it can be a very difficult message for some people to hear. And an even more difficult message for some people to live. And a very dangerous message to some people who don't want you to hear it because it will invalidate what they've been saying for years. And no one likes to be discredited. Look at what happened to Jesus. He was killed for preaching his message. He said it best – The good news, this life transforming message, will fall on to three types of people: some will ignore it; some will try to embrace it but be cut off by others; and a small few will be able to cultivate the message and transform their lives.

The key is to know that the message is counter-cultural. It goes against what we have been raised to believe. Yet it is completely in line with what you know in your heart. Every day you long to hear this message. You seek it out. And you are empty without it, constantly searching for something—anything—to make you whole again. Your soul understands the message completely, your heart desires it more than anything, but your head and ego can get in the way. And other people will try to stop you from living out this message because they don't—or can't—understand how to live it out in their lives.

## Take a Moment

- ⇒ What does it mean to be accepted in a community?
- ⇒ Are there people in your own life who are on the "inside"?
- ⇒ Who are the "outsiders" in your life?
- ⇒ What would happen if you broke down one of the barriers in your community?

# 3

# WHERE'S CHRIST IN TODAY'S CHRISTIANITY?

*"You see, there is no good tree
that gives rotten fruit,
nor, on the other hand,
any rotten tree that gives good fruit.
Indeed, each tree is known by its own fruit...
The good person brings forth good
from his heart's good treasury,
and the bad person, from his bad treasury,
brings forth bad, because his mouth speaks out
what his heart is brimming over with."*

The Good Word According to Luke,
Chapter Six

You can tell what's important to an organization—any organization—by what the people within that organization spend the most time on. What do the people talk about? If you go to a bakery, chance are you'll hear people talking about bread. If you go to an automobile manufacturer, you'll see pictures of cars, hear people talking about cars, probably even see some cars. Whatever takes up the most time, effort, energy and resources are what defines the organization. You could say that whatever that thing is, that's their "god."

Churches also name their god according to their lived priorities: their actions. You can tell what's important to a church community, what defines the community and the people within it, by what the church—and the people within it—spend the most time, effort, energy, and resources on. When you go about your day, what do you spend the most time on? Who do you spend the most time with? How do you feel about that? When you go to your local church, or you talk to another person, particularly a Christian, about their beliefs, what do they talk about? Who do they talk about? What do they spend their time on?

Often, I find myself looking through different books on Christianity or listening to Christian ministers or pastors. The most amazing thing is that they rarely ever talk about, spend their time or resources on, Jesus and the gospels. I've spent months listening to pastors who talk about gay marriage or abortion almost nonstop. I understand that many people find these issues important enough to talk about. Why would a pastor or minister spend more time talking about one issue as though Christianity is a moral code or set of social rules, instead of talking about Jesus as a life-changing spiritual catalyst? In California, for example, Christian churches spent countless hours and literally millions of dollars in their effort to stop gay people from getting legally married in the state (when the state had already allowed them to marry legally). But, how much time, effort, energy, and money do those churches (and the people within them) spend cultivating their relationship with Jesus? How often did those churches talk about Jesus during their campaign? Now, I'm not talking about "Jesus is on our side and he hates you." I'm talking about the original message of Jesus, promoting love among all people.

In books, movies, teachings, and from the pulpit, Christians spend an awful lot of time talking about the Old Law (Leviticus) or Paul's letters. If I were to label many of the churches I've been in who call themselves Christian—based purely on who they talk about the most—I would say that these churches are some form of Paulianity. Paul said this. Paul said that. Paul told us to do this. Paul set the rules for how we live, what we believe, and how we worship. I recently read a book that claimed to turn Christianity on its head by offering a view of "Jesus and nothing else."

When I read the book, I was shocked (not really) to discover the author writing about Paul. The author explains that Christianity really begins with the crucifixion of Jesus and that Paul is our model. And page after page of "Jesus and nothing more" was filled with everything except Jesus.

For just a little test, try visiting your local Christian church a few times. Time how much the pastor talks about Jesus directly versus how much time the pastor spends talking about anything other than Jesus, or says things like "Paul tells us Jesus is about this." If you're feeling a little more brave, ask the pastor to talk with you individually about Jesus. See how much time the pastor explains the actual words and actions of Jesus directly.

Instead, you're likely to hear lots of talk about Paul, other letter writers, other books in the Bible, the Old Testament, etc., etc., etc. You may even hear about other people not even mentioned in the Bible. And you'll hear that you need to make a personal relationship with Jesus, that you have to decide to be saved, and that what it means to be saved is to follow all of the rules that Paul mentions in his letters or something out of the

Old Testament.

Now, imagine a church built on only the Four Gospels.

## I Came to Fulfill the Scriptures

Ask any Christian leader about what drives their beliefs, and more often than not, you'll hear some brief comments about who Jesus is and what he did. Then you'll hear about everything else in the Bible except Jesus. Rarely do Christian leaders define their churches through the words and actions of Jesus.

This book is not a treatise on the nature of Jesus as God and man. Christians believe Jesus is God. Neither Paul nor any of the Apostles fall into this category. So, as God, the words and actions of Jesus are not only the beginning of the Church teaching, they are the totality (the beginning and the end) of it. Everything else is just interpretation, the "old law" that has been fulfilled, or an attempt by a person or group to add to what is already perfect and complete. That is the nature of God: perfect and complete.

And yet, Christian leaders attempt to fill in detailed answers to specific questions as though Christianity is a "laundry list" of theological answers to every question that can be developed—and that a specific "universal answer" should be found for every question under the sun and applied to everyone. The teachings and actions of Jesus indicate otherwise. God's law is written on our hearts; it is a living, changing, and adapting the principle of love. It is not a universal set of dogmatic rules to follow in every conceivable situation. It is an approach to living with God and others that requires a focus on heart and soul.

Pastors in American Christianity seem to feel the need to "have all the answers." When we examine the words and actions of Jesus, we find that when he was questioned on specifics, he gave the answer, but often the questioner did not want to take the time to work out what the answer meant. So the questioner would repeat the question or ask for a clarification like "What do you mean, Jesus?" And Jesus would inevitably provide a clarification that was so extreme that no human being could possibly live up to it. For example, Jesus said to be faithful in our relationships. What does that mean? Well, it means to be faithful in our relationships. We know what it means when we are in a relationship. In some instances, it means leaving a relationship because of abuse to be faithful to the relationship we have first with ourselves and God. In other instances, it may mean remaining true to a partner in business or love when the opportunity to turn your back arises. In any case, what it means to remain faithful in every relationship will vary for each and every relationship and in every new present moment within that relationship. To be faithful means to be vigilant within that relationship. It means more than just "not cheating;" it means being devoted to the relationship and to the other person in it.

But the questioner wanted more. What does that mean, Jesus? How can I be faithful? I don't want to be responsible for the answer, so you tell me. And Jesus responds, "if you even look at another person with lust, you have committed adultery." Wow. That's Jesus' way. In other words, we know the answer, and it is always about personal responsibility. We are responsible for remaining true to our authentic selves. We are responsible for knowing our hearts, minds, and souls. We are responsible for doing the work, taking the time, and walking the walk. And whenever we want to abdicate that responsibility to someone else by asking "But what does it mean for me? I want you to provide the answer to my problem so that you can be responsible for it and I don't have to be." Then, you will not like the answer because it will be too much to bear.

In other words, if you want Jesus—or your pastor or anyone else—to be responsible for your life by telling you what to do, then the answer from Jesus is "you must be more than the perfection that God created, you must live up to my standard, which is unreasonable because I am not you.

"If I am going to be responsible for your actions by providing the answer, then the answer will be something that takes responsibility away from me and puts it back on to you."

So, Christian leaders look elsewhere for the answers because Jesus remains silent on so many specific issues. His silence, they interpret, means that Jesus didn't answer those questions and opened the door to someone else to provide them, generally Paul. Or they look to the "old law" when it is convenient. Or they look to someone completely different. And in that process of looking to someone other than Jesus for the answer, they miss the point entirely. They make the Christian life unbearable, unreasonable, and overly complicated. Instead of cultivating a present-moment relationship with God who speaks to us even to this day, they try to apply someone else's answer.

But that is not how Jesus, who is God, taught us. The law, he says, is written on our hearts. We are connected to the Source of All in every moment. And we deny that living relationship every time we go outside of it. We betray God when we deny our perfection and we deny Jesus when we search for answers in the "old law," or the prophets, or the apostles, or the pastor of my local church. Those may be tools that God uses in our present-moment reality, and they can give us comfort, but they are ultimately not the answer. The answer always lies in our heart.

Jesus summed the answer up in one word: love. Specifically, love God, love yourself, and love others. No other law matters more. And all of the laws flow from this one Law. Any law that does not flow from One Law is fulfilled, it is complete in the eyes of God and no longer matters to us.

Growing up, I attended religious education at my quasi-conservative neighborhood Catholic school. I also went to "vacation Bible camp" at one of the evangelical churches in town for a summer or two. My "religious" education also included my parents' involvement with the "charismatic" movement popular among some Catholics in Southern California, a few years at a high school seminary, a degree in Religious Studies, and way too many Christian conferences, youth groups, professional development events, retreats, and probably a few potlucks thrown in over the years. Additionally, I learned from religious and spiritual leaders, as well as my friends from many different religious traditions.

Throughout all of this, I learned ultimately one large lesson that seemed to underlie everything else: I was broken. And because I was broken, I needed to be fixed. Everyone, of course, had their own version of what being "fixed" meant: being "born again" in evangelical Christianity, repenting for my "sins," attending a particular church or religious group regularly, or something else entirely. The point was always the same. I am sinful, not perfect, less than what I'm supposed to be (by birth) and that I needed to spend my life fixing myself.

I'm not sure where this basic belief that we're broken comes from, although I have a few good ideas of how and where it got started. But the fundamental belief rears its head in funny ways. Guilt, for one. Many comedians and religious folk joke that their own religious upbringing "owns" guilt. I was taught that guilt was good. It meant that I was somehow in touch with what God was telling me. And I further learned, whether it was implicitly or explicitly taught, that I should not be happy with anything that is sinful. And it turned out that almost everything about being a human being is, somehow, sinful. "Love the sinner, but hate the sin." How many of us have been told that at some point in our lives?

I learned that my passions, desires, body, thoughts and

feelings were all sinful. I ultimately learned to hate myself because I could never live up to the perfection that was expected of me or that I expected of myself. Oh, I tried. I tried every way I knew. But it just never worked out quite well. Oh, it might work for a week or two, even a few months, but ultimately, I would never be perfect in the eyes of those religious and church leaders who explained how easy it was to experience God's joy and peace in my life by following a set of man-made rules and regulations.

Here's the funniest part of the whole thing: I very rarely heard life's lessons as voiced by Jesus. There was always some other source in the Bible or in church history who trumped Jesus himself. St. Paul consistently ranked higher than Jesus in the "person to actively quote when making a religious, particularly Christian, point" category. In one breath, I was told "You can't get to heaven except through Jesus." And in the next breath (if one was even taken—sometimes it was said in the same breath), "And Paul told us … That's what it means to follow Jesus."

Now, I have nothing against Paul. He seemed like a decent guy. He said some pretty impressive stuff, and he was very influential in spreading the Christian message throughout the world. Some would say that he defined Christianity as a religion. The trouble is, he's not Jesus. And he did manage to say some things that appear to contradict Jesus' very own words and actions. His intentions were good, but we would do well to skip over him and start (and end) with Jesus.

One of my friends once said that if he were the devil and wanted to destroy Christianity, he would make people uncomfortable with the human body. After all, how could Christianity remain true to the teachings of Jesus if the followers are uncomfortable with being human. Jesus is God in human form. And if "being human" means being sinful or imperfect, than how can we believe in a God who would take human form?

And so it seems today, and for much of Christian history, the idea of being human is equated with "a necessary evil." While the language may sometimes indicate otherwise, the implicit understanding is that humanity is something to be controlled, suppressed, or denied. Without getting into theological or historical analysis of this (there are many great books on the subject already), none of this is directly due to anything that Jesus said or did. Instead, it came about as people interpreted Paul's teachings to his followers throughout history. Jesus is remarkably silent on the vast majority of positions that Christianity has come to embrace as dogma in some form or another.

But Jesus did say something interesting. "Deny yourself. Take up your cross. And follow me." For Jesus himself, his cross was his destiny. Today, most Christians interpret our cross as a burden we must bear, something to overcome in our lives. And yet, if we understood our cross to be our destiny, that which we were born to do, the statement has a much more profound—and life-changing—meaning. Often, the thing that keeps us from fulfilling our destinies is, well, ourselves. We get in the way. Our egos stop our souls dead. We believe it is up to us to determine our life's path. But if we stopped for a moment, we would realize that, however we came to be who we are today, we have everything we need for a specific purpose on this planet.

God provided us with a unique set of gifts and talents to achieve our soul's desire. The ego operates to protect us, and so it operates out of fear. Like a well-trained security guard, our egos are ever vigilant against any damage—or potential damage—in our lives, regardless of whether that damage is real, perceived, or imaginary.

So, to embrace our destinies, we must often embrace love over fear and learn to let go of fear, which is to deny the ego. We must learn to say to our private security guard, "I've got this. It's ok. Back off." We must deny it. Only then can we see the path laid out for us and follow it, one step at a time, to wherever it may lead. And even then, we are only given enough path to handle in any particular moment. We rarely are ever given the entire path; we are given what we need to walk our path.

## Take a Moment

⇒ Try reading one of the gospels, preferably a direct translation instead of an interpretative translation, and ask yourself what beliefs you've been taught that conflict with what you're reading.

⇒ How would you act differently if you lived out the words of the gospel?

# 1

# WHAT JESUS REALLY SAID ABOUT GOD

*"You see,
God so loved the world
he gave his only son,
so that everyone who believes in him
would not be lost
but instead have everlasting life.
God didn't send his son into the world
to condemn the world,
but so the world could be saved by him."*

The Good Word According to John,
Chapter Three

So, by now you're asking yourself, "How can I be fertile ground?" How can you be one those people who hears the message, believes it, and cultivates it in your life? That is, hands down, the top question people ask me. And the answer is simple to say but requires some effort. I'm talking about the same sort of effort that it takes to brush your teeth in the morning. Initially, it took some trial and error to get it right, but now today you are able to exert that same amount of effort without thinking about it.

What is the secret way to open your heart and mind to this life transforming message?

## Believe it

It is that simple. But believing it is easier to say than it is to do. And this goes back to the social dynamic of human beings. While we fancy ourselves as independent thinkers who don't go with the crowd, every scientific study seems to indicate otherwise. We are built as "creatures of habit who generally do what is accepted by the group."

And so, even though the first step is to be open to the message when you receive it, the challenge is to remain a believer beyond the resistance that the group of people surrounding you will exert. And this doesn't just apply to this message. Think of people who diet to lose weight, start a fitness regime, attempt to quit smoking or give up an addiction. In the vast majority of these circumstances, people experience a "push back" from their family, friends, co-workers and others in their lives.

Think of the dieter. It seems once you begin a diet, people try to sabotage you at every turn: "Oh, it's OK. Just one dessert won't hurt. It's a special occasion, we're celebrating. You don't want to ruin the celebration by not having a piece of cake, do you?"

One of the rules that any doctor who works with addicts will tell you is the importance of removing yourself from the same group of circumstances in your life.

God created some universal systems that deal with these

sorts of situations. The challenge is to embrace the laws and use them. You will find that as you begin to transform yourself, some of the people around you will obviously be supportive of you and others will not. You will know who is not. And it is up to you to allow them to leave your life gracefully.

And you will find that just as quickly that as you allow those people to depart from your life, God replaces them with others who are completely supportive of "the new you." It is your choice how you feel about this process. You can rejoice that the people and circumstances that held you back are no longer in your life and replaced by those that help move you forward. Or you can resist the changes and retain your old life. The choice is completely up to you.

Now, back to the answer. It was simple. "Believe it," I said. "Sure," you said. But how do you do that? Look at other things that you believe. For example, you believe that the sun will come up every morning and that it will set in the evening. You believe this because of the unique combination of education and experience that has told you so. But, remember that this belief was not always held the same way it is today. It is a belief that has changed, as our scientific knowledge has changed.

But back to that belief about the sun. How does it feel to believe it? How much effort does it take? Do you think about it every day? Do you worry about it before you go to bed? No. You accept it and probably don't think about it at all.

And that is how to believe it. You have to accept it at a deep level. You have to reject the opposite to believe it. For some people this is fairly easy. For others, this can be more difficult, depending on how in touch with your own conscious and subconscious mind you are.

## Take a Moment

⇒ Ground yourself in the present moment. Many religions

and sacred traditions associate God with The Breath of Life:

⇒ Find a safe place.

⇒ Set a timer for 15 minutes.

⇒ Get comfortable. Sit or lay down ... doesn't matter.

⇒ Close your eyes and shift your focus to your breathing.

⇒ Allow your thoughts to move through you without engaging them. Simply acknowledge the thought and allow it to pass.

⇒ Allow your mind to clear while you focus on your breathing.

# 5

# WHAT JESUS REALLY SAID ABOUT PEOPLE

*"Leaving aside the commandment of God,*
*you keep the tradition of the world,"*
*And he said to them,*
*"You're very good at setting aside*
*the commandment of God*
*to establish your own tradition."*

The Good Word According to Mark,
Chapter Seven

**You will know them by their fruits.**

When I see Christians taking actions that they claim in the name of the Law, I am always amazed at the number of people who end up being hurt, or those who end up feeling betrayed. Think of what Christianity has become in America.

In a recent survey, Christians in America were three times more likely to approve of using torture in "the war on terror" than non-Christians. Torture?! There is little difference between the Christians protesting at the funerals of gay people, holding signs that say "God hates fags" and the Christians who brutally murdered Matthew Shepherd for being gay. In California, Christian churches spent millions of dollars to take away the right of gay people to get married. The fruit is the same, even if one is a more ripe version than another.

My point here is not to engage in a political debate. There is no debate. Jesus was clear on these issues. "Love your enemies and pray for those who persecute you" doesn't leave room for torture. And Jesus' commands regarding marriage consistently focus on people needing to remain faithful, loyal and true in their relationships. He was never fixated on gay people or gay marriage. And when given the opportunity to mention it, Jesus makes something very clear: God hates inhospitality—more than anything else—enough even to destroy a city over it.

That's something that is important to note here. When we strip away Paul, the Epistles, Revelation, and the Old Law, we are left with a different focus. The fruit of Christianity in America could best be described as a loud argument. Christian churches seem to be overly fixated on a few issues that are not central to the message of Jesus. But perhaps the real fruit of these churches is the millions of people who have been turned away from God, told they were too damaged or evil, and made to feel like "Jesus doesn't want you." For these millions of people, and other onlookers, Christianity has almost no resemblance to the words, actions, or love of Jesus.

I've noticed a fascination with "The Suffering Christ" that has always been interesting to me. One of my friends pointed out that Mother Theresa told us that we should take on the example of Christ by suffering for others. (For the record, I don't think Mother Theresa was advocating that we should suffer for others. I think she advocated living a simple life in service to others, but not that such a life should be one of suffering.)

I think here's where Christians have completely missed the boat. Jesus suffered. Yes, but there's the rest of the sentence, and without the rest of the sentence, it is easy to completely miss the point. Jesus suffered *so that we don't have to*. In other words, when Jesus said, "my burden is easy and my yoke is light," he actually meant it. Life in our earthly existence is supposed to be a joy. Life should feel easy. Unfortunately, for many people, an easy life must mean that something is wrong: they aren't working hard enough, they aren't doing enough, they can't have good things while other people have none. And yet, Jesus said that the poor would always be with us, and that we should focus our attentions on our relationship with God. Again, not to the exclusion of others, but our sole purpose is to first love God so that we can love ourselves and others. It is through cultivating a loving relationship with God that we are able to find peace, joy, and abundance. And through the love of God, we learn to love ourselves within the same breath.

We cannot love God and hate ourselves.

That loving relationship is easy and carefree. When you are your authentic self in relationship with God, you have no excuses, no burdens, no stress. You know that God works in partnership with you creating your path as you walk along it. And the path feels effortless. When obstacles come in the way, you know that they are not obstacles but steppingstones along your path. You know that you always have everything you need. Anxiety has no place in such a relationship. Anxiety comes from being apart from God, from trying to live outside of that relationship.

## Take a Moment

⇒ Do something that you enjoy.
⇒ Enjoy it. Laugh. Be in the moment.
⇒ How can you bring that joy to every aspect of your life?

# 6

# WHAT JESUS REALLY SAID ABOUT SALVATION

*And he said to him,
"I promise you,
Today you will be with me in paradise."*

The Good Word According to Luke,
Chapter Twenty-Three

You may be questioning this whole idea of perfection. I mean, who considers a short temper part of perfection, right? But that's just the point. We spend our lives being taught to run away from who we really are. We're told that it's just plain wrong to be human and we should strive for something "better than human." But God didn't make us better than human. God made us human. For a reason.

Being human, being fully how God made us, is perfect. Sure, there are rough edges and bumpy spots. That's the point of being human. Those rough edges and bumpy spots are part of the perfection.

And if we celebrate who we are, how God made us, if we can look in the mirror and see the person God created instead of the person we've learned to settle for (and possibly dislike on one level or another), we open ourselves up to the perfection that God has given us.

Those things that we sometimes look at as "bad," and therefore "sinful," aren't necessarily either. One of my friends said that if he was the devil and he wanted to destroy the message of Jesus—the message of God's love—he would do it very simply. He would make people uncomfortable with being human. If we are uncomfortable with our human nature, then we cannot be fully comfortable with a God who chose to embrace humanity.

Let's face it: Jesus farted. He was a human being. And many people believe he was also God. But does God fart? Could God do that? Take a Moment to consider your reaction to the first sentence in this paragraph. Did you cringe? Did you have a little bit of a "did he really just say that?"

Why?

You should ask yourself that question a lot more. Why? Why do you think that? Why are you afraid of that? Why do you do the things you do? Why do you have the dreams you do? Why do you act on your instincts? Why do walk away from your dreams? Why do you hold yourself back? Why do you have the friends you have? Why? Why? Why?

Ultimately, the point of the exercise is to move you through to your unspoken beliefs. To get you to question what it is you do, why you do it, and why you haven't questioned it before.

Jesus said, "Let those among you who are without sin cast the first stone." And yet I see people casting stones every day. It seems we would rather live other people's lives than focus on our own. The simple beauty of what Jesus really said is this: our own lives are worth living fully. God has given us dreams and the talents and unique abilities to pursue them. To run toward them without giving it a second thought.

And yet we allow the noise and distractions to get the better of us. Our parents, friends, relatives, co-workers, and acquaintances all tell us who we should be and how we should get there. But they do not know what is in our hearts. They do not speak for God. God speaks directly to your heart. There's a direct connection there.

That connection is free from guilt and shame. God loves us completely and without regret. We are challenged to see ourselves the same way. Loving yourself is actually easier than you think, if you are committed to yourself. I'm not talking about arrogance and selfishness. I am talking about self-interest and self-love. Recognize that God will take care of everything if you take care of yourself. Take the time to listen to your heart.

And if it's been a while, you may need to be still that much longer to reconnect to it. But you must reconnect, for God lives there in the stillness of your heart, mind and soul.

But here's the other great part of all of this. God will also take care of everyone else. You are not responsible for them. You are responsible for and to yourself. Now, this is never an excuse to be mean or inconsiderate—quite the contrary. Through the recognition of your own self-worth, you are also free to see the worth of everyone else. Everyone has value, even if you do not recognize it immediately.

Let me say that again: *everyone has value.* And you must honor that value in others as much as you value it in yourself.

How often do you have friends (or perhaps you yourself) who go on a diet or try another self-improvement program? Think about those experiences for a moment. When you're out with a friend who's dieting, are you one of the people who says, "It's okay. A little dessert won't hurt you." Why is it that when someone is trying to improve themselves, other people find it necessary to derail their self-improvement program?

A truly supportive person knows their own self-worth is not dependent on diminishing another person's worth. Salvation is for everyone. There is not a limited amount of salvation, just as there is not a limited amount of any blessing, success, prosperity, or abundance.

As you walk the path, others may not be supportive. Let them go. Others may challenge you. Let them go. Others may not understand. Let them go. It is not for you to judge them or to keep them in your life. God's path will become clearer and clearer to you every day, and you should follow it.

But you always should recognize the value of others, and you should never stand in their way. Instead, be supportive of them and their dreams—especially when you do not understand them. There will be many people who do not understand you, yet you will want them to be supportive of you.

## Take a Moment

⇒ Look in the mirror. Study yourself for a moment.

⇒ Name one aspect of yourself that you like.

⇒ Repeat this process each day, naming something new that you like about yourself.

⇒ How many days can you go without repeating the same aspect of yourself that you like?

# 1

# WHAT JESUS REALLY SAID ABOUT RELIGION

*And in the course of his teaching he said, "Watch out for clerics*
*who love walking around in their robes*
*and everyone saying hello to them downtown,*
*and their seats in the front of churches*
*and at the head table of banquets,*
*who wolf down the houses of widows*
*and make a show of praying at great length.*
*They will receive an extra condemnation."*

The Good Word According to Mark,
Chapter Twelve

## Don't tell anyone, show yourself to the priests.

Jesus commanded that his followers spread the message. If anyone rejected the message, they should dust off their feet and move on to the next town.

Today, some Christians have taken the command to evangelize and mixed it with the message of perceived brokenness and turned it into something completely new: Evangelical Christianity. This new form of Christianity today, particularly in the United States, compels its followers to believe and do several things:

- Recognize that they are broken and convert to their brand of Christianity to be fixed.
- Recognize that their individual salvation is directly tied to how many other people they can "fix" through conversion.

This combines to make for a very zealous lot. And so, now we have a cadre of people who feel compelled to "spread the good news," meaning convert every nonbeliever they see. Because they believe that nonbelievers are fundamentally more broken than they are (or "as sinful as they once were before they were saved"). This really has the opposite effect of the real message of Jesus.

This variant of Christianity holds to the "you're in or you're out" mentality. By seeking to view everyone as an outsider who has not specifically agreed to follow their specific interpretation of what it means to be a Christian, they create an inherent polarization within Christianity and among people in general. In short, you either love them or you're going to hell, in their estimation.

But, if we return to the authentic teaching of Jesus, this viewpoint is quite wrong. If everyone is saved by virtue of God's love and grace, and Jesus fulfilled the "old law" that commanded specific actions to define yourself as a member of the "in group," then we need neither follow the old law nor comply with a specific set of laws.

After all, Jesus said that the law was made for us, not that we were made to follow the law. And so it is that those who truly believe in the authentic message of Jesus—that they are indeed saved, loved and cherished by God exactly the way they are—will naturally live a different sort of life. A life of love, service, and dedication to themselves, their family and community, to strangers, and to God. There is no distinction for these people between how they treat God and how they treat a stranger—for everyone they meet holds the same high value and is loved and welcomed in exactly the same way.

This is an unconditional welcome, and an unconditional love. The same love God has for us that God demands we have for each other and for ourselves. Jesus identified this as "the greatest commandment."

And yet, we find many "Christians" today who outright reject this message in favor of a slightly modified version that favors those they deem worthy.

This is a direct challenge to the authority of Christian pastors and leaders everywhere. And one I am sure they would discourage among their followers in favor of their interpretation of the "law."

Now I can already hear the computers whirring up, the pencils being sharpened, and the giant placards being made in protest of these very words. And that is precisely the point. Some Christians will hear or read this message and believe that it goes directly against everything they've ever thought.

## They Will be Afraid of it

But why? Why do Christians engage in such blatant displays of un-Christian behavior? Personally, it makes no sense to me why any Christian would feel that everyone else should believe—and by believe, I mean "act"—just like themselves.

For some reason, Christians believe they will somehow be

held accountable for other people. But Jesus is pretty clear that not only will they not be held accountable for other people, they will be held accountable for how they judge other people. Most Christians I've met who embrace evangelical Christianity are able to do some pretty startling mental gymnastics to justify their judgments of other people and their actions relative to "strangers."

And, quite frankly, that makes me sad. Because I wonder just how much they can really experience the love and happiness that God intends for all people if they are so concerned about other people all of the time. If they are literally consumed with the need to convert other people to "save them" from whatever damnation and punishment they think will be doled out. All the while failing to recognize that they themselves are passing some pretty severe judgments that—according to Jesus—will form the basis of how they are judged by God.

In other words, God will judge us according to the mirror we attempt to hold up to other people. And so it seems to me that the best way to live your life, according to the real teachings of Jesus, is to avoid judgment whenever possible because, quite frankly, we do not know what is in someone else's heart, mind and soul, and therefore our judgments of them always will be wrong.

But if we completely believe that we are not broken—and other people are just as "not broken" as we are—then we are compelled to live a different life ... A life filled with peace, joy, happiness and abundance ... a life that rejects comparisons and competition in favor of compassion and community.

After all, where does most anger, frustration and sadness come from in our lives? I think that when we identify it, we notice a startling pattern. We get angry because we are unhappy with ourselves. We think we should be different or better somehow—a bigger car, more money, better looking, have people treat us differently, etc.

We get frustrated in traffic because we think other people should drive differently. We get angry in relationships because we think our partner should act or be different towards us. We find ourselves unhappy when our lives don't live up to a perceived image of how it was supposed to be.

Instead, the message of Jesus seems to indicate that it is our attitude about all of this that needs to change. And the fundamental change in our attitude needs to be one of acceptance of what is. And not just acceptance really, but a celebration of what is. Even when it doesn't look exactly the way we think it should, it is perfection in the eyes of God. It is our job to see that perfection whenever possible.

We find perfection in the ordinariness of everyday life. Instead of assuming that we, as individuals, must be the completion of all perfection, we must look at ourselves within a much larger context. We are perfect in ourselves because we are part of a larger perfection that includes all of the world. We have a part to play in the larger universe. We were individually created not to be the completion of all things by ourselves, but to lend our gifts and talents to become part of the perfection that is the universal whole.

## Take a Moment

- ⇒ In the Hawaiian culture, there is a process called ho'oponopono. Basically, it is a process of "cleaning memories" and "repairing relationships." Ultimately, it is the process of repairing the relationship with yourself.

- ⇒ Find a quiet place where you can be still. Get comfortable but be fully present.

- ⇒ Close your eyes and envision yourself bathed in love and light.

⇒ Allow the first person or image to come to mind. Repeat the following phrases with intention:
- I'm sorry.
- Please forgive me.
- Thank you.
- I love you.

⇒ Remain in the love and light. Embrace the image, allow your mind to move to the next person or image. Repeat the process. You are not speaking these phrases to the individual or the image but rather to the universal consciousness.

# 8

# HOW TO LIVE AN UN-BROKEN LIFE WITH YOURSELF

*So pray like this:*
*"Our Father in the skies,*
*Let your name be sanctified.*
*Let your kingdom come,*
*May your will be seen on the earth,*
*just as in the sky.*
*Give us day by day the next day's bread,*
*And forgive our debts the same as*
*we forgave the debts that others owed us.*
*And do not put us to the test,*
*But snatch us from the Evil One's clutches,*
*Let it be so."*

The Good Word According to Matthew,
Chapter Six

## Missing the Mark

For years, Christians have understood sin as a separation from God, a willful action on the part of human beings that damages our relationship with Jesus. And Christians have further understood that we are sinful by nature. This misunderstanding of the Adam and Eve story ultimately underlies almost all other Christian teaching. We're broken, we learn at an early age, and even after God fixes us through baptism, we're still likely to continue to be broken for as long as we live.

But the actual word that is translated as "sin" in the gospels actually means "missing the mark." It is used to describe when an archer shoots an arrow toward the target and misses it. The truth behind this word—the one Jesus and the gospel writers actually used—means that Jesus understood that we are fundamentally good. Our nature is not that we are separated from God, but that we are constantly moving toward God. While we move toward God and our intention is always for the good, we sometimes miss the mark and do the wrong thing or make a mistake.

This is not a fundamental flaw; it is a process of growing on our journey. We are perfectly created beings who seek re-union with our creator. And on our journey, we get sidetracked and sometimes make choices that result in the wrong outcome. Sin, the intentional choice to separate ourselves from God's love, is about intention, not outcome. We can never separate ourselves from God's love. Nor do we desire to do so. Instead, our intention is to do the right thing, and we sometimes miss the mark.

## Faith the Size of a Mustard Seed

Jesus said we have to faith the size of a mustard seed. One of the smallest of all the seeds that grows into one of the largest of bushes. But what does that mean, exactly, to have faith? Is it simply to believe? Yes. You have to believe. But believe in what? How do you "believe"?

The answer is simple, the process can be more complex.

Which would have the greater impact on your life right now?

- Knowing that someone deposited $1 million into your bank account yesterday.
- Knowing that someone will deposit $1 million into your bank account at an undetermined date in the future.

If you're like me, chances are knowing that someone deposited money into your bank account yesterday (that is, it has already happened) would have a greater impact on your life today. After all, not having the money until some date in the future is not particularly helpful to you at this very moment.

This exact paradigm exists in our lives. Christians struggle with this. I know many Christians who believe that Jesus indicated that we will be "saved" at some point in the future if we do a certain list of things. The trouble with this thinking is that it neglects a fundamental word choice that Jesus made. You see, when Jesus was talking about "salvation," he used the present perfect tense. Not "will be saved" but "are saved."

It's the difference between saying "You will be a millionaire" and "You are a millionaire."

Basically, the same words, but the impact on your life is tremendously different. In one instance, you can spend the money now and in the other you can't.

Jesus wanted us to know that we can already "spend" God's love, grace, and salvation. We already have it in the bank. This is probably different from what you may have been told. I like to think of it as the best worst kept secret in all of Christianity—

perhaps all of religion. This knowledge is why the message of Jesus is so life-transforming and so often misinterpreted. I'm not sure why some people hold on to the idea that salvation has to be earned. I hear Christians tell me in one breath that Jesus already saved me and then in the next breath tell me that I still need to be saved. This has never made sense to me. In fact, it makes less than no sense to me; it is absurd.

Which brings me to the point: did you know that you already have God's love in your life? Did you know that God already gave you peace, joy, and abundance? Did you know that you are graced?

But, just like a million dollars is meaningless until you actually spend it (After all, just because I have a million dollars in the bank doesn't mean my life is any different—the difference is in my ability to spend it.), so is God's love. God's love is meaningless until you spend it—on yourself and others.

So, how will you spend God's love today?

## Consider the Lilies

My favorite passage in all of scripture is Jesus telling his followers that God loves them more than anything, that He always will be there to protect, provide and care for them.

Consider the lilies of the field, he says. They do not want for fine clothes, yet they are clothed in all of God's splendor. Consider the birds of the air, he says. They do not want for shelter or food. And yet, how much more does God love you that God has already provided for all of your needs before you even ask?

And yet, when we put this into the context of the rest of Jesus' teachings, we recognize that God put in place spiritual and physical laws that govern the universe—and that when followed, yield great abundance, peace, and joy for those who live within them.

One of those laws that is often talked about these days is the Law of Attraction. If you've read the book or watched the movie The Secret, then you are aware of the discussion.

This universal law works this way: believe it and you will receive it. The trouble I've seen with the way the law is discussed these days is that this spiritual law is being promoted as a means of acquiring material wealth with little discussion about the spiritual nature of the law itself. Since it is grounded in the spirit, the results will be—and must be—spiritual in nature. And yet, much of the talk does not bring enough attention to this important component of the Law of Attraction and its context within all of the spiritual laws. But it makes sense that this law, like all others, has a purpose within the greater universe of our existence.

Jesus was talking about this law when he said that we do not need to worry about how God will provide for us. Instead, we just need to know—to believe, to have faith—that everything will provided for us.

This reminds me of a story. A close friend of mine received some money unexpectedly. The money was legitimately hers, and it was directly deposited in her bank account at a time when she could use it. She just wasn't expecting it to happen when it did. What was her initial response? Did she praise and thank God? Was she filled with joy? Did it bring her peace, a sense of the abundance that God provides?

Her immediate response was to contact the bank to launch an investigation into how the money arrived. Who sent it? Why? Was it all a big mistake? When would it be taken away? This is how she lives her life – always hoping for something good to happen and then wondering what went wrong when the good is brought to her. I do not think she is a very happy person. I do believe she experiences happiness, but I'm not sure that she holds happiness in her heart. It seems she is always looking for how she will be punished in this life, all the while praying to God to take the worry away.

I wonder what her life would be like if she trusted in God's love for her. I wonder if she really believed that God will always be there to take care of her as God always has been there. Does her life always look exactly the way she thinks it is supposed to look? Probably not. In fact, I would venture that no one's life looks the way they think it is supposed to look. And yet, when we trust in God, believe in the abundance and live in the present moment, we are never disappointed. In fact, the opposite happens, God takes care of everything in ways we can never dream of or imagine.

There is wondrous joy in the experience. But it takes letting go as much as it takes the work of believing. That is the beauty of God's plan for us. God loves us so much that the world was created to protect and provide for us automatically. There is more energy, more food, and more resources on this planet than we could possibly use for thousands and thousands of years.

And yet, we worry and fret. We start wars over the precious resources. We stop imagining and creating with what God has provided and fight over what we think it is supposed to look like. Instead of celebrating that we are given everything we need, we become greedy, wanting more and more. We not only want what God has already provided for us, we want what God has provided for everyone else so we can hoard it and control it—never trusting in the sustainability of the divine

In your life, you probably experience this sometimes, either as the person wanting more than you need, or as the person being denied what God has given because someone else has taken control of it. Except God still provides in ways we can never fully understand. Like my friend, who received money deposited into her bank account when she wasn't expecting it.

At a time when "there's just not enough money to go around for everyone" and "the economy is so bad." Imagine that. Pennies from heaven. Hallelujah! Praise God! Thank you for every blessing on earth that we have received, are receiving, and are about to receive.

I'll take the clothes off the back of lily any day.

## Take a Moment

Create a Blessing Book:
- ⇒ Be intentional about choosing a notebook and pen.
- ⇒ Before you go to bed, find a blank page and write 10 things you are grateful in your life, or that are a blessing to you.
- ⇒ Focus your attention on those while you drift off to sleep.
- ⇒ Repeat this process every night.

# 9

# HOW TO LIVE AN UN-BROKEN LIFE WITH OTHERS

*An expert in the Law of Moses stood up
and asked Jesus a question
to see what he would say.*

*"Teacher," he asked,
"what must I do to have eternal life?"
Jesus answered,
"What is written in the Scriptures?
How do you understand them?"*

*The man replied,
"The Scriptures say,
'Love the Lord your God with
all your heart, soul, strength, and mind.'
They also say,
'Love your neighbors as much
as you love yourself.'"*

*Jesus said,*
*"You have given the right answer.*
*If you do this, you will have eternal life."*
*But the man wanted to show that*
*he knew what he was talking about.*
*So he asked Jesus,*
*"Who are my neighbors?"*

Jesus replied:
As a man was going down from Jerusalem to Jericho,
robbers attacked him and grabbed everything he had.
They beat him up and ran off, leaving him half-dead.

A priest happened to be going down the same road.
But when he saw the man, he walked by on the other side.

Later a temple helper came to the same place.
But when he saw the man who had been beaten up,
he also went by on the other side.

A man from Samaria then came traveling along that road.
When he saw the man, he felt sorry for him and
went over to him.
He treated his wounds with olive oil and wine
and bandaged them.
Then he put him on his own donkey and took him to an inn,
where he took care of him.
The next morning he gave the innkeeper
two silver coins and said, "Please take care of the man.
If you spend
more than this on him, I will pay you when I return."

*Then Jesus asked, "Which one of these three people was a real neighbor to the man who was beaten up by robbers?"*

*The teacher answered, "The one who showed pity."*
*Jesus said, "Go and do the same!"*

> The Good Word According to Luke,
> Chapter Ten

## A Man was Walking Along the Road

Like all good teachers, Jesus used vivid stories to illustrate his points. And like all good stories, they are meant for a specific audience, in a specific time, at a specific place, and with specific culture references and techniques. And the preferred story of Jesus' time for his audience was something called a parable.

Parables are unique in that they are clearly meant to explain a specific lesson and provide guidance for how to live. In Jesus' day, these stories were meant to be spoken to an audience, and so they followed a strict formula. The audience knew who to pay attention to and how to apply the story to their own lives because of how the story was told. It was also easier for a storyteller to pass along a remembered story because the formula was important. Get the formula correct and the story tells itself.

So, what does this mean for us today? In some cases, it means that we've misinterpreted stories and their original meaning is all but lost to a contemporary audience. That meaning has been replaced by one that seems to be similar but has dramatically different consequences for us in applying its meaning to our lives.

Let's look at the story of *The Good Samaritan*.

It seems to be a pretty straightforward answer to the question. But, when we put this story back into the original context and formula of oral story-telling, we get a startlingly different interpretation that Jesus' audience would have picked up on right away. For them, this story was shocking and unexpected. But, why?

The message seems deceptively simple. We should take care of those who are less fortunate than ourselves. We should be moved with pity and act.

But there's much more to it than that. You see, Jesus' audience would have recognized that the very first character mentioned is the most important, and therefore the one they should identify with. Yes, the audience would have wanted the priest or the temple helper to stop and offer assistance to the dying man, but they would have also recognized that the Law of Moses would have prevented them from doing so (as would the "expert in the Law"). However, they would have wished beyond everything else that the man from Samaria would not stop and help him.

People from Samaria were very much disliked by the community that Jesus was talking to. They were so disliked in fact that not only would someone not want to help a Samaritan, they also would not want to be helped by one. What did it mean for someone who was left on the side of the road half dead to be helped by someone? It meant that you literally owed your life to them. And you had to repay the debt.

But what would it mean if you were saved by someone and you only had a vague idea of who that person was? How do you repay the debt you owe to them? After all, the man who was left half-dead on the side road could not know exactly who the person who helped him was. To whom did he owe his life? All he would know from the innkeeper was that a "Samaritan man" brought him and left enough money to take care of him. And so, he would owe his life to every Samaritan man that he met in the hopes that he would be able to repay the debt eventually. To do otherwise would be wrong.

His audience understood this. The debt of a life saved is a serious debt indeed. They would also very much never want to owe their lives to a Samaritan, let alone to every Samaritan. And yet, in this story, they were being challenged beyond what the law required. They were being asked to treat every Samaritan not only as a friend, but as someone to whom they owed the debt of their very own life.

The man asking the question would also not like this answer. Because it challenged him beyond the letter of the Law. It challenged him to think of the law as something bigger than anything a human being could design. He was forced to think of a Samaritan, someone who he would normally think of with disgust, as someone not only of great worth, but of more worth in the eyes of the Law—and therefore God—than someone who was following the Law.

All of this is significant to us today. But why? What does it matter that Jesus told a little story about being good to people who are suffering?

When we apply the context to our lives in today's world, we make a startling realization: those people who we don't like, who we do not value in our lives—those are the people to whom we owe the greatest debt of all. How different would the world be if we embraced this as a way of life? If we treated every stranger as someone to whom we owed our very lives? Would we live in fear? How would we treat the people we meet by chance throughout the day? What choices would we make in these situations? How would we be transformed?

Imagine what a world that would be. That is the kingdom of God that Jesus talked about. And that is significant to us in more ways than we can count.

Try it for one day. Treat everyone you meet as though you owed your life to them. See how they treat you in return. At the end of the day, look back on those moments and you will see the face of God.

If you can't try it for a day, then try it for an hour. If you can't try it for an hour, then try it with just one person.

## Take a Moment

True gratitude is a blessing. Try saying "thank you" to every person you interact with today. If you can't say it aloud, then say it in your heart, mind and spirit. You don't even have to know what you're thankful for, just be grateful. See what happens.

# 10

# WHY IT STILL MATTERS

*"If you forgive people for stepping out of line,
your heavenly father will forgive you too."*

*"Don't trouble your heart about what you will eat and drink
and clothe your body with."*

*"Don't judge, so that you won't be judged;
you will be sentenced to the same
sentence that you sentence others."*

*"So everything you want people to do for you,
you do the same for them."*

The Good Word According to Matthew,
Chapters Six and Seven

## Some Seed Fell on Fertile Ground

I was driving with some friends of mine in the car the other day. Both of these friends are fairly well-versed in the ways of theology and religion. Both are very familiar with the message of Jesus as it is taught and passed on by most religious leaders today.

But both were caught completely off guard when I told them what the message of Jesus really was. They were both silent for a while. Both understood the message, knew that it felt right, but both had trouble with it. Why?

Because it was so different, so life-changing, that it turns everything they were told completely on its head. And it is so fundamentally easy to get. But people have trouble embracing the message because it requires a change. To believe it, and live it, it requires thinking about yourself, God, and other people in a completely different way. In that way, it is foreign. It is not a habit of thinking that we can easily adopt; although the message is easy and simple. It can be a challenge to live out.

After all, how do you shake off years and years of thinking one fundamental truth only to realize that the truth was backwards? It can be very disheartening. It is possible to subject yourself to blame, to think that you somehow should have gotten it sooner. That you, of all people, should have known it. This is a truth that you should never have had to hear from someone else.

Because you already knew it. Your heart told it to you over and over again. Your spirit lives with this every day.

But as we grow, we learn to turn a deaf ear to our heart and we learn to tune out our spirits. We learn to do what everyone else around us does. We are social beings. And we like to be part of the group. We like to know that we are accepted in the community. We like to know that we belong. And if no one else in the group is believing, acting, saying, thinking, or doing a particular thing, then it can be very difficult to embrace a new way of thinking and being.

Some people will definitely reject you for it. But they are not rejecting you. They are rejecting the message.

After all, how can it be true? Because if it really was true, wouldn't everyone be living it out every day?

And that, quite frankly, is why the message is so amazing. That is why thousands of years ago a small group of people said, "Yes. That is exactly right. That is the message I hear in my heart. That is what I know in my soul. Yes. Yes. Yes."

That group of people were so excited about the good news (gospel) that they told literally everyone about it. And some of them were killed for it, others suffered for it, and others were able to spread the news further and further until it was embraced by nearly the entire population of the "Western World." And why today it is embraced by literally billions of people.

But the message has been distorted over time. And the fundamental meaning has been lost. As Christianity became the "official religion" of the political leadership, the message changed. The message became about defining who was "in" and who was "out." But this time, the message was attributed to Jesus himself.

The message became this: **"You are bad. You need to be saved. Jesus can save you. But you need to be part of the community of believers to be saved. Here are the rules for being part of the community. Follow the rules, get your friends and family to follow the rules, and don't associate with someone who does not follow the rules. Do this, and you will be in. If you are in, then you will be saved."**

But this message, while similar to the original message of the religious and political leaders of Jesus' day, is just as wrong. It is fundamentally wrong because it starts with the wrong idea. But it does support the need for some people to retain power and control. It feeds the need for some people to feel that they are better than someone else. And in that, those people have understood the message of Jesus from the wrong perspective.

## Forgive Them, for They Know Not What They Do

Remember the two friends I was driving with? Well, as we were discussing this, the conversation went something like this...

Me: Jesus brought such a simple message that we are saved here and now without needing to do anything to earn that salvation.

Friend #1: You're right. I was listening to this pastor who said that while we're all imperfect, we need only accept Jesus to reach God's perfection.

Friend #2: Yeah. We're saved because of what Jesus did.

Me: No. That is exactly wrong...

You see, Christians have been saying this:

- You're broken (sinful).
- You need to accept Jesus as your personal savior.
- Then Jesus will "wash away" your sinfulness and you'll be saved.
- Only Christians will be saved, and it is the obligation of all Christians to try to save others by converting them to Christianity.

Of course, this is a simplification, but the basic idea is there. But here's why it is **exactly wrong:**

Jesus said-

- You are not broken.
- You are perfect because God created you and loves you.
- You do not need to do anything to earn this love or to earn salvation.
- You are saved right now (not something that happens

in the future).

- Those things that you think are imperfections are really part of God's perfection.
- If you really believe, you will live a transformed life.
- Share this news with everyone you meet through the example of your life.

This is life-transforming. Imagine looking in the mirror and recognizing that you are a perfect, loved child of God. That there is nothing you can do to drive God away from you. That God has already saved you. That you are awash with God's love.

And now imagine that when you go out into the world, you recognize that everyone else that you meet is just as loved, just as perfect, just as saved as you are.

No one is cast out of the community because no one is outside of God's love.

If you take that knowledge into your heart, mind, and soul... If you believe it with your entire being... What would your life be like? How would you go through your day? How many "enemies" would you have? How often would you be angry or upset at another person? How much more understanding would you be?

And what then would the world look like? How would nations relate to one another? How would we treat immigrants to our country? How would we treat strangers?

What a world that would be!

When we come to this realization, then Jesus' message has its full impact. Sit with this idea for a while. What difference does believing this message have in your own life? What would your life be like if you fully embrace it?

## Take a Moment

Every time you catch yourself in a state of chaos or confusion, immediately pause, take a breath, relax your body as you exhale, and focus on feeling a "big hug." You Are Loved.

# 11
# APPLYING THE WORD TO TODAY

Let's examine some contemporary topics that often come up in Christian circles. We'll view these topics within the context of the spiritual truths presented by Jesus.

## Focus: Politics

Christians in America today have focused a lot of their attention on trying to influence politics. The "Religious Right," as it has been called, was started to create a Christian political majority. I'm not sure exactly where the basis for this movement comes from, as there's nothing in the Bible, especially in the gospels, that would promote using political force to create a Christian society.

Quite the opposite seems to be the case. When we examine the gospels for evidence of Jesus' teachings regarding politics and government, we find a couple of startling concepts:

- "So give Caesar's things to Caesar and God's things to God." (Matthew, Chapter Twenty-Three)

- An emphasis on honoring the intent of the law.

If Jesus was concerned with keeping the spiritual and the political separate, it seems only fair to note that perhaps Christians—the followers of Jesus—should honor that same concern. The founders of America had this keen understanding in mind when they wrote the First Amendment, which created (for the first time in human history) a government that completely separated religion from politics.

Doesn't it seem fair, then, to say that if we live a life aligned with the teachings of Jesus, the law holds no power over us and we do not desire to change the government to bend to our will or impose our beliefs on anyone else? Instead, we create a Christian society through our example of being Christian to one another.

Jesus was big on example and small on words. There are many instances where Jesus points out the hypocrisy of leaders. But what leaders was Jesus concerned with?

Many people of the time were expecting a messiah who would transform the political landscape and create a Jewish world. This was especially true of the religious leaders of the day, who were more focused on the power they could wield within the community. Jesus was, on the contrary, never concerned with politics. He was not concerned with convincing people to change the government in any way. Instead, Jesus was a religious activist, calling for the transformation of the Church through an emphasis on a personal relationship with God.

We are called to live in God's grace, and to recognize that our example will call others to live in God's grace as well. As our individual lives are transformed, our society is transformed as well—through God's grace. We cannot vote God into the hearts of the citizens living in our country. We cannot legislate God's grace into the life of our nation. The transformation takes place within the individual, and spreads out into the community, and ultimately the country.

Jesus talked about remaining faithful and loyal in all relationships. He also talked about honoring the spirit of the law, specifically God's law. He noted that, first of all, the people asked for the law—the law was not imposed on humanity—that was never God's intent. Secondly, he noted that the law was made for human beings—we are not subservient to the law. This very statement seems to indicate that as human beings grow and develop, so must the law and our understanding (and implementation) of it.

I know many Christians who hold the understanding that God is "unchanging" and so the law is also "unchanging." Except, taken in the context of Jesus—who is God—we have a different way of relating to God (living and changing) as well as the law (the law is written on our hearts, not in stone). That is a real challenge for modern Christians, as well as Christians throughout the ages.

It's easier for us to seek out a divine, universal, unchanging law that applies to everyone and make every good effort to ensure that everyone is following the same law. But, that is exactly what Jesus was not concerned with. His teachings are very clear: we are responsible for ensuring that we follow the law that is written on our hearts. We are responsible for cultivating the loving relationship with God, ourselves, and others. And the law indicates that two things are important to this pursuit:

1) The actions that flow from this loving relationship are "reflective," that is, we treat others the way we want to be treated. And we will be treated the same way that we treat others. (It works both ways.)

2) The intentions and thoughts that we hold in this loving

relationship are non-judgmental. We do not judge ourselves or others. For any judgments that we issue will be placed upon us.

This is actually easier than it sounds, but it means abandoning some seriously ingrained false ideas that we have passed down from generation to generation. And it means that true Christians are not concerned with changing the laws of man, but with honoring the laws of God. How much effort do Christian churches exert today to change laws to reflect their own moral standards?

This is a very dangerous movement, not because of the moral standards themselves, but the methods being used to promote them actually create the opposite effect. And, as we know well by now, the fruits of an endeavor tell us whether it is within God's law or not. Instead, we should embrace more fully the idea that Christianity is a human way of being and not a political system.

Christian political movements—like The Moral Majority or the Religious Right, or whatever other name you'd like to place on it—work in opposition to God's plan. They do not yield the proper fruit, and that is something that Christians need to take a serious look at. It is not the "nice words" that matter, it is the impact that actions have on other human beings. Jesus never got physically or outwardly angry except in one stand-out instance—how people were treating God's house. Specifically, Jesus was upset that the religious leaders had allowed the temple (the Church) to become a place of the world instead of a place for God.

Think of Jesus overturning the tables at the temple the next time your local church engages in a drive to increase donations. Why? Is that what Jesus meant? More importantly, where is your donation to the church going? Yes, churches survive on donations, but they do not need to be wealthy. There is a difference between cultivating a community's sacred space and building a 50,000 square foot mega-church with coffee shops, gyms, giant auditoriums, and other features that are built around human personalities—religious leaders—who should be moving everyone's focus to God and, therefore, to the good works that God asks of us.

## Focus: Value of Life

For Christians in America, there are few issues of greater importance than abortion. Rightly so. Abortion is the ending of a human life. There is no debating that. The current approach for churches is to push for legislation outlawing abortion for everyone and in every circumstance. Unfortunately, Christians lose their moral authority very quickly in the area of claiming to honor human life. And this is reflected in the ongoing debate regarding abortion, particularly in American society.

The challenge Christians face is very complex, as is the issue itself, and I'm only offering a cursory discussion about the topic here. But I want to examine the issue within the context of the whole topic of the value of human life. "Respect Life" committees exist in many churches, and yet those committees and the people on them—through their actions and the actions of the Christian community as a whole—do not truly embody the idea of respecting life. Instead, these people and organizations have one goal in mind: make abortion illegal.

The intent is right: save human life. But, the point is wrong. As we know from previous discussions in this book and elsewhere, Jesus commands us to love our neighbors and to NOT judge them. We cannot know what is in their hearts and minds, and we cannot make moral decisions for them. Each individual is responsible for his or her own choices, words and actions—and ultimately for the fruit of their lives.

Jesus rarely admonished people with "don't do this" statements. Instead, Jesus offered positive statements of what we should be doing. And, so I agree that we should honor and respect life. All life. And that we should cultivate a community that respects life as well. But, for many Christians, that isn't the case. The immense effort spent on telling other people how to live their lives and what moral choices they should and should not make by codifying them into law is exactly the wrong approach. And this approach comes from the underlying Christian perspective that people are fundamentally broken, that regardless of what you do, they will make the wrong choices unless you provide appropriate punishments for it.

But there's definite trouble with this point of view, and it does not reflect Jesus' understanding of humanity and how people work or how they should make choices as a community. Let's look at the fruit of this approach with regard to abortion among Christians. As a teacher, I used to be responsible for various parent-student nights. One favorite activity that students and their parents appreciated was called "Walk Your Convictions." The idea was simple. A line was drawn down the center of the room, and participants were asked to walk to one side if they agreed with a statement or to the opposite side if they disagreed with it. No one could stay on the line. The object of the exercise is for people to learn to listen to opposing viewpoints to understand them better. And so, a few people from each side would volunteer to explain why they walked to their side of the room. The one rule of the exercise is that no one is permitted to comment on the opposing viewpoint, only to express their own viewpoint.

From doing this exercise over the course of many years, I noticed some interesting patterns in terms of who walked to the agree and the disagree sides of the room. Inevitably, most Christians would walk to the agree side in terms of believing that abortion is wrong. But, on all "respect life" statements, most Christians would walk to the disagree side of the room. For example, most Christians agree that the death penalty is morally ok.

I want to break just that one comparison down for you. Most Christians believe this:

1) Abortion is always evil.
2) The death penalty is not evil.

Here's the trouble with this, and why those two statements, taken together, are completely unchristian when applied to a society. Abortion is, and always will be, a personal individual choice that one or two people make, and therefore remains the moral responsibility of only those one or two people. The fact that a society allows people to make choices that may or may not be moral does not create any moral responsibility on the part of any member of that society as long as the choice is not mandated to any individual, and the actions are not carried out compulsorily by the state, society, or government. In the instance of abortion, someone who chooses to have an abortion and perhaps those people who facilitate the actual process, bear the moral responsibility for their actions. Again, as long as those actions are not compulsory on any of the individuals involved. And make no mistake about it, the decision is not a cavalier one for anyone involved.

On the other hand, the death penalty is a societal decision; it is the "people" who are making the moral choice to terminate a life, and then the "people" united together carry out the action. Sure, perhaps only a small group of people is actually involved in the decision to end the life and to then carry out the action. But those people are acting on behalf of everyone in the society, and so the moral responsibility for the terminating of the life of a prisoner lies with the entire community. In other words, the difference between abortion and the death penalty in terms of moral responsibility is that the people who are morally responsible for an abortion are only those people actually involved, while those who are morally responsible for the use of the death penalty include every member of the society.

Given this, I am always shocked that Christians care more about judging another person's moral choices then in being responsible for their own, especially when those choices are made by others on their behalf. This is also true for warfare. When the government, acting on behalf of the people, engages in activities that result in the intentional loss of human life, every member of that society bears the moral responsibility for those actions.

And yet, how often does the Christian community speak with one voice when everyone is morally responsible for the death of another human being in these circumstances? Christian leaders have led their flocks astray every time they have convinced them that we need to pass laws outlawing abortion in every circumstance and at the same time support the death penalty or any unjustified war of choice.

But what would it look like if Christians were actually living out God's commandment with regard to this topic? Quite frankly, the time, effort, energy and money spent on anti-abortion legislation would be channeled into providing prenatal care, early childhood education, after school care, easier access to adoption and foster care, improved education, universal healthcare, and so on. In addition, Christians would examine the fruit of comprehensive sex education programs that actually decrease the spread of STD's and prevent unwanted pregnancies from happening in the first place. Christians would seek ways to help women who've had abortions find peace and healing in their lives without judging their past choices, and encouraging them to move forward in God's love and grace. Christians would know in their hearts that they cannot force another person to make a particular choice, nor should they. And most importantly, Christians would refrain from judging anyone who's been in a position of facing this issue firsthand, as we can never know what is in another person's mind, heart, or soul—and we will never be held responsible for that unless we pass judgment, in which case that judgment is reflected back to us.

## Focus: Sexuality

Another topic of great fascination for Christians is sexuality. Holding up picket signs at funerals, passing laws to make same-sex marriage illegal, forcing abstinence-only education into schools, condemning anyone outside of what seems to be a narrow definition of appropriate sexuality. To what end? Jesus hardly mentions sexuality, and he never mentions it as a negative except to indicate that we should be faithful in our relationships.

When Jesus mentions Sodom and Gomorrah, he does not mention sexuality at all—instead he focuses on the inhospitality of the people of those cities. Inhospitality, it seems, was one of the greatest sins Jesus could imagine. The sin of not welcoming the stranger, of not respecting "outsiders," is grievous in the eyes of God. And, yet, it seems to be the single sin that Christians are the best at displaying in their own communities. Every day, Christians engage in behavior and practices that are, at best, inhospitable without even realizing it. Entire churches are built around the premise that you're either "in" or you're not. Complex initiation rites and rituals and processes and classes and "formation" are used to keep outsiders out and insiders protected against the "evildoers" in the world.

Even the notion of evangelism takes on an inhospitable form. Instead of spreading the Good News, some Christians engage in a form of religious ambush by approaching random strangers on the street to verify their "salvation status," condemning them to hell unless they listen—and act—upon the words of the stranger. I've been approached by several people engaging in this behavior in my lifetime, and when I responded that I was "saved," they reacted in disbelief, questioning me further "Who saved you?" "When were you saved?" "How do you know it worked?" "How can you be saved if you aren't part of particular church?"

And that brings us back to the fundamental issue presented in this book: Christians have somehow received the idea that people are fundamentally broken and need to be repaired, over and over again, until eventually it sticks. But the gospels present us with a God who loves us without condition—so much so that God has already saved us even if we don't recognize it. The price for salvation has already been paid, and our salvation is not only in heaven, but in the here and now. And yet, some Christians continue on about their business of trying to save people, or validating other people's salvation, as though that is what God intends for us, like there's a secret "salvation club" and God commands us to go around checking people's membership cards before we can even talk to them. And if they don't have a membership card, then it's our obligation to drop everything else and recruit them.

And so it is with sexuality. When we look at the gospels and use them as the core of the Christian message, we find very little—if anything—to construct an understanding of sexuality that even remotely resembles the one presented by some Christians today. Instead, these Christians focus on two primary sources for their understanding of sexuality: Leviticus and Paul.

Leviticus, which should be obvious to Christians, represents the old law—the law that is completed and fulfilled in Jesus and therefore no longer applies. Christians have done this with just about every prescription within the Old Law—eating shellfish, selling children into slavery, stoning people in the town square, and so on. Except with sexuality, or more specifically homosexuality.

In the days of the Old Law, it was common for women to be treated as property, and as such, women were subject to the power and will of men—including when and where and how they would have sex. If a man demanded sex of his woman, she was obligated to provide it as long as she wasn't unclean (and in that case, he shouldn't be demanding it while she was unclean, as that would make him unclean). But men, who were the power center, retained their free will and dominion of others, except over other men. So, a man was prohibited from "taking" another man the same way he would take a woman. That violated the principle of men being autonomous equals within the power structure of society. Any Christian woman today who quotes Leviticus should really re-think whether or not that's the Gospel message of equality she wants to be promoting. But, as I said, the Old Law no longer applies, and Christians do well to consider it fulfilled.

On the other hand, there's Paul. I want to make something very clear, and I'm sure this will offend Christians everywhere: Paul was not, is not, and never will be the Totality of God. Jesus, on the other hand, was, is, and will continue to be God. And so, in the "do I choose Jesus or Paul" debate when they contradict each other, I believe the proper Christian thing to do is to choose Jesus, because he's God, and Paul is not. Having gotten that out of the way (yes, it really is that simple and there's no sense in arguing it any other way since to do so would be to question the authority and divinity of Jesus), we can move on to understanding how to place Paul within the construct of Christian teaching.

Let me offer a little analogy. Paul was simply a founder of Christian communities. He was a missionary traveling throughout the area teaching the Good News to whoever would listen. And once he set up a small community, he would leave someone in charge of it (the local pastor), and then he would move on. Sometimes, though, the community would have issues that they couldn't readily address within their ranks. So, off with a messenger to dispatch a note to Paul who would then respond in kind with a note of his own replying to the specific questions being sent to him from that community. The community would treasure the letter and read it aloud every now and then as a way of retaining contact with their founder, Paul. It was a letter from an old friend. Over time, as Christian communities came together to form a common organization, they began to swap their letters, eventually forming books that were later edited together into what we now know as the Bible through a fairly long—and sometimes politically charged—process.

Imagine today if the emails from the founder of your church were printed together into a book and distributed to everyone as though they formed the foundation of the very teachings of your faith that should be applied to everyone. That doesn't make any sense, any more than it makes sense to treat Paul's individual letters to specific communities dealing with specific issues of their day as more important than the gospels themselves. Think about it for a moment: How much weight does your church place on Paul? How many times is Paul quoted and treated as the ultimate authority over even Jesus himself? And when Paul contradicts Jesus, how many times does your church so easily dismiss the teachings of Jesus in favor of Paul's words?

These are serious questions that demand a serious examination by today's Christians. It is exactly wrong to treat Paul as God, for Paul was not, is not, and never will be God. So, if we do the proper thing and place Leviticus and Paul in their appropriate context, we gain a new understanding of sexuality within the human experience. Sexuality is not something about which we can so easily create—nor should we—black and white moral pronouncements that apply to everyone. Instead, we should follow the example of Jesus by separating the spiritual from the political, embracing all people as children of God, and seeking to understand that we are not God so we do not have the capacity to judge others when we do not walk in their shoes.

Yet the Christian argument is made that all families (all marriages) must look identical, or the world will collapse, God's mighty judgment will come down on anyone who accepts and loves other people even when they do not understand or choose to condone their behavior. (There is a difference between loving and participating in.) Massachusetts is a good example of this. Last time I checked, the state was not struck down by God in a mighty display of forceful vengeance. No plagues. No loud thundering voice from the heavens. However, when I look at any area where Christians are actively engaged in preventing same-sex marriage, I see communities torn apart, people divided into loud arguing factions, protests and anger, and violence against others. These communities are not suffering these awful effects because of same-sex couples, they are suffering because of the actions of Christians. And, we already know from Jesus, that we will recognize a Christian community by its fruits. What are the fruits of these protests and political movements? Are the hungry being fed? Are the prisoners being visited? Are those without clothing and shelter being protected? Jesus never said that the sheep and the goats would be separated based on their stance on homosexuality; but Jesus does provide a very clear path to salvation for those who believe

## Focus: Environment

Christians have always held that human beings are the stewards of God's creation. Jesus certainly held true to this principle. Today, though, Christian teaching on this subject has been hijacked by something far more sinister: politics. The Christian mantra is that "climate change is not caused by human beings" so we therefore have no need to change our actions quickly.

But the fact of the matter is that human beings have dramatically altered the environment on planet earth, and we continue to do so. Christianity, According to Jesus, is about personal responsibility as well as social responsibility. It is irresponsible to suggest that people do not need to take every reasonable action to protect the environment. In fact, the only reason people have for failing to protect the environment are purely selfish: businesses want to engage in their practices to make the highest profit without regard for stewardship, people want to eat and hunt and fish without regard for sustainability, individuals want the most comfortable and easiest life without the effort of working to take care of the world around them.

The entire argument—any argument—against proper stewardship and care of the environment is, quite frankly, an anti-Christian argument. It doesn't matter whether or not there is global warming. It matters that, as Christians, we are called to the highest responsibility with regard to our environment. If we know that dumping litter on the ground poisons our oceans, then we have a moral obligation to not litter—and to proactively remove other people's litter as well. If we know that nuclear waste can't be stored safely, that burning coal damages our air, and that fossil fuels impact our world negatively, then we have a moral obligation to pursue other forms of energy and to stop using those sources of energy that are damaging our world.

The issue surrounding climate change really is as simple as that. Oh sure, we can go on and on and on ad nauseam arguing about who is to blame, or what scientific finding is valid, or we can recognize our own moral responsibility and take whatever actions are necessary. The point here is not to argue about the past and to try to refute the science, but to accept what's going on and make the changes necessary in our lives. Change your light bulbs to energy efficient ones. Turn off lights when you're not using them. Choose more energy efficient options when you have the choice. Seek out ways of existing that lower your impact on the world. Recycle. Eat a little less meat. None of these things will end your life or make it dramatically less comfortable. And it's just plain stupid to not do anything.

My point is this: God made us responsible for the world, and we have to take that responsibility seriously. For example, did you know that water will become the most scarce resource on the planet? What are you personally doing about that? More importantly, what will you do if your community runs out of water and there's not enough for yourself and your family? It is a distinct possibility if we don't work together in the manner God intends for us. Yes, God provides for our needs, but our fear and ignorance can cause us to destroy the very gifts that God provides.

## Focus: Science

I find many aspects of the discussion of science and religion to be rather amusing. First of all, no one's salvation lies in believing that the earth was created in seven literal days or that Adam and Eve were the first humans on the planet. Neither will anyone be condemned to hell for believing that God could begin and maintain a process of creation that includes evolutionary biology and dinosaurs, or that the universe is billions of years old. Let me say that again: Nothing about this debate or the accompanying beliefs on either side will either get you into heaven or place you in hell.

Jesus brought forth salvation for all people who cultivate a loving relationship with God, others and themselves. (Love God and your neighbor as yourself.) Jesus was never concerned with the past. He focused on the present and the future, knowing that they were intrinsically linked. Every present moment creates a future moment, and how we live in the present is more important than what we think might have happened in the past. In fact, the only thing our concerns for the past can do is harm us if we're not careful—in that some beliefs we can harbor in this arena can lead us to place judgments on ourselves or others that we will be held accountable for.

I think that if Christians viewed the gospels as, well, "gospel" and everything else as secondary to the gospels, then the battle between Christianity and science wouldn't exist. Because Christians would not hold on to beliefs that, quite frankly, aren't central, or even really important, to embracing God's love and grace. Instead, Christians should ask themselves, "Does this matter to my relationship with God?" And then they should ask, "Does this really matter to my relationship with God?" Whether God created the world in seven days or created the process of evolution, whether the first human beings were named Adam and Eve or something more complex happened over millions of years...do any of those things really matter to our relationship with God? Or, more importantly, do we allow differences in our convictions to get in the way of creating loving relationships within our communities, creating judgments, divisions, and meaningless debates that destroy our adherence to the greatest commandment?

Since we are not broken and don't need to be "fixed," then we can shift our understanding from one of fear to one of love.

Instead of being afraid of science, knowledge, and new understanding, we can embrace the gifts of our intellect and curiosity and know that science and religion form two sides of the same coin. Science is not a perfect end; it's answers are no less perfect than a strict adherence to a translation of a translation of a translation of an ancient text. I know there are Christians who will silently—or very publicly—disagree with me on this (and many other points). And that is what I'm talking about, the level of yelling and argumentation among Christians is in complete opposition to the gospel. You can't be a true Christian, believe that Jesus is God, and contend that God meant for us to be confused by the message, and so we should argue about it among ourselves, all the while attempting to amass as large a following to our point of view as possible.

## Focus: Salvation

As I've talked about throughout this book, many Christians have a distorted view of salvation. I'm not sure exactly how the theology makes sense to Christians who believe it, but it goes something like this...

Even though Jesus said that he came to save people, that God loves us (here and now), that we live in God's grace and compassion every day and that we merely need to live in God's love, many Christians still believe that there is a "price" we have to pay to earn God's love and salvation.

I've never understood the disconnect. Either God loves us and has already saved us through the death and resurrection of Jesus or not. If God has not done that, then Christianity as a religion is built on false claims. If God has already done that, then why do Christians act like that hasn't happened yet?

The answer lies in what happened after Jesus died and rose. The reality is that other people (Paul, some of the apostles, some later church leaders, some political leaders, etc.) got involved. Because of their own human frailty and imperfection, they couldn't personally accept the fundamental message of Jesus: you are loved right here and now, just the way you are, because God is perfect and demonstrated that perfect love for us through the person of Jesus. Instead, the message got slightly twisted, taking on the cloak of a "private club."

This private club mentality says, "God loves those people who are in the club, and rejects those people who are outside of the club. So, you should join the club and follow our rules."

But that's just it. We shouldn't follow any rules laid down by men. We should follow God's rule. And God's rule is simple: Love God and Love One Another. Period. There is no more to God's law than that. So, it seems that the challenge of Christianity is in learning to love. If we examine the gospel message a little further, we discover that Jesus recognized that human beings are built around a fundamental desire to love, and that loving starts with loving one's self before loving another, or even love God. And so Jesus expands on this message to teach us how to love: Do unto others as you want them to do to you. Treat others the same way you want to be treated.

Do you want other people to protest your lifestyle? Do you want others to condemn you to hell because of your beliefs? Do you want others to constantly try to convert you to their way of thinking? Do you want others to engage in pre-emptive attacks on your community? The list goes on and on. How do you want others to treat you? Jesus tells us the result: you will be judged the way you judge others. In other words, how you are treated every day is directly related to the way you think about and treat others.

Think other people are going to hell? Then, I hope you enjoy being there as well, because you have sealed your own fate based on your judgment of others. It is as simple as that. Jesus didn't sugarcoat it. Jesus didn't alter the message to be more acceptable to people. Jesus made it plain and clear. And that frightens those Christian leaders who use fear to retain power within the Christian community. If Christians read, understood and lived the gospel—and nothing more—then Christian leaders' authority would be undermined. There would be no "us" vs. "them" to talk about. There would be no focus on eternal damnation to scare people about. There would be no aggressive cornering of people to demand that they accept Jesus the way their church demands. Instead, Christians would live lives worthy of the founder: lives of love, compassion, and nonjudgment.

Only then, can Christians experience the salvation that Jesus talked about. Only then, can Christians enjoy God's love.

## Focus: Evangelism

Evangelism is the process by which Christians go out into the world and ask a simple question: "Have you accepted Jesus Christ as your personal savior?" This question is meant to lead to a discussion in which the responder to the question is ultimately led to a conversion experience by accepting Jesus. My own trouble begins like this: Someone comes up to me and asks The Question. I respond with a yes (mainly because it is easier than engaging in an entire theological conversation with someone who has a single-minded purpose). The person than engages in a process of verifying that I am, indeed, going to be saved.

This is the part I don't understand. The person who has asked me if I accepted Jesus rarely accepts my answer and instead insists that I really haven't accepted Jesus because I didn't do it at his/her church. This begs the question I raised earlier: Clearly the goal of most evangelicals is not to "save people" but instead to increase attendance at their own individual church.

If we go back to the gospels themselves, we see that evangelism is spreading the Good News through example. And remember that the Good News is not the question "Have you accepted Jesus Christ as your personal savior?" The Good News is that God loves us and that, through Christ, we are already saved.

The Good News that Christians are challenged to spread to all the world is that God loves you, has always loved you, and has saved you from the beginning of time. The "choice," if there is one, is not to accept Jesus, but to live with the confidence of God's love. Think back to the million dollars. How would you live your life if you knew you had a million dollars in the bank versus waiting for a check to arrive? It's the same with every other aspect of our lives. How would you live your life if you knew beyond a shadow of a doubt that you were loved, cared for, and "perfect just the way you are"?

Let it be so.

# ABOUT THE AUTHOR

Stephen Fofanoff is the host of the Soul.Pizza podcast, studied religion at Gonzaga University and has a master's degree in organizational leadership from Mount St. Mary's University. As an author and personal coach, Stephen endeavors to improve the quality of life of the people he reaches. Stephen has helped people around the globe to realize their ideal lives. He resides in the Pacific Northwest with his artist husband, as well as Ponzu and Alex, their two shelter cats.

www.ingramcontent.com/pod-product-compliance
Lightning Source LLC
Chambersburg PA
CBHW052114110526
44592CB00013B/1602